Space Mysteries

Mysteries of Alien Life

T0386560

Margaret J. Goldstein

Lerner Publications ◆ Minneapolis

Lerner Publications Company
An imprint of Lerner Publishing Group, Inc.
241 First Avenue North
Minneapolis, MN 55401 USA

For reading levels and more information, look up this title
at www.lernerbooks.com.

Main body text set in Adrianna Regular.
Typeface provided by Chank.

Editor: Andrea Nelson **Designer:** Martha Kranes

Library of Congress Cataloging-in-Publication Data

Names: Goldstein, Margaret J., author.
Title: Mysteries of alien life / Margaret J. Goldstein.
Description: Minneapolis : Lerner Publications, [2021] | Series: Searchlight books—space
    mysteries | Includes bibliographical references and index. | Audience: Ages 8–11 |
    Audience: Grades 4–6 | Summary: "Scientists have sent messages into space
    hoping that aliens will find them. But we may have already received messages of
    our own. Young readers will learn about the current scientific mysteries surrounding
    extraterrestrial life"— Provided by publisher.
Identifiers: LCCN 2019047564 (print) | LCCN 2019047565
    (ebook) | ISBN 9781541597372 (library binding) | ISBN 9781728413846 (paperback) |
    ISBN 9781728400853 (ebook)
Subjects: LCSH: Life on other planets—Juvenile literature.
Classification: LCC QB54 .G59 2021 (print) | LCC QB54 (ebook) | DDC 576.8/39—dc23

LC record available at https://lccn.loc.gov/2019047564
LC ebook record available at https://lccn.loc.gov/2019047565

Manufactured in the United States of America
1-47841-48281-2/20/2020

Contents

Chapter 1

GREETINGS, EARTHLINGS

TV, films, and books are full of fictional alien life-forms. Some people even claim that aliens have visited Earth from outer space. But does life really exist beyond Earth? Scientists say it's possible. They want to find the facts.

The *War of the Worlds*, a science fiction novel by H. G. Wells, is one of the earliest books about aliens and humans. It was first made into a movie in 1953.

Despite their many differences, hummingbirds and flowers are both examples of living things.

Tree of Life

What does it mean to be alive? Scientists define a living thing as something made from one or more cells that can reproduce, grow, move, and respond to the world around it. Earth's living things can look very different from one another. Tiny bacteria are living things. So are green grasses and towering trees. Humans, sharks, hummingbirds, geckos, and bees are living things too.

Scientists think life first formed on Earth about 3.5 billion years ago. They think energy from the sun combined with water, carbon, hydrogen, and other substances to cause a chemical reaction. The chemical reaction created a living cell. It grew and reproduced.

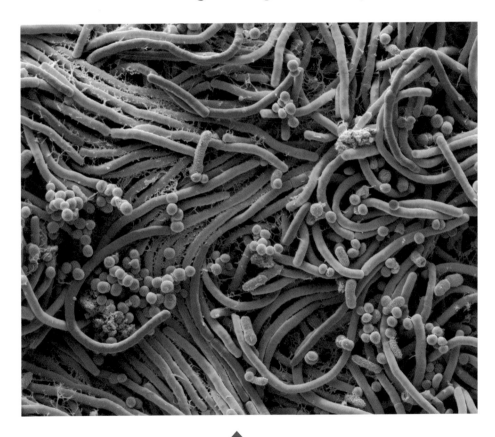

BACTERIA ARE EXAMPLES OF LIVING THINGS MADE UP OF ONLY ONE CELL.

Some living things, such as flowers and insects, are made up of many living cells.

Over time, Earth's living things became more complex and took new forms. Modern-day Earth is home to millions of different kinds of living things.

Is Earth the only place with life? If life formed on Earth, it's possible that it could form on another planet, in another solar system, or in another galaxy.

Chapter 2

CLOSE TO HOME

Scientists are looking for life elsewhere in our solar system. Water is fundamental for life on Earth. Plants and animals are made mostly of water. Water carries nutrients and other vital substances through the bodies of living things. If a planet has liquid water on it, it may have life too.

Scientists think that planets with liquid water could have life on them.

Curiosity is looking for signs of life on Mars.

Mars has water ice covering its north and south poles. Scientists believe liquid water once flowed on its surface. Mars also has carbon, hydrogen, and oxygen, which are also important for life on Earth. The National Aeronautics and Space Administration (NASA) has sent spacecraft to Mars to look for signs of life there. In 2019, one of the spacecraft, the *Curiosity* rover, found large amounts of methane on Mars. On Earth, some living things produce methane. The methane is another sign that Mars could be home to life.

Scientists believe Saturn's moon Enceladus could have the ingredients needed for life.

Other places in the solar system have ingredients for life too. Between 2004 and 2017, the *Cassini* spacecraft took pictures of and gathered information about Saturn's moon Enceladus. The data showed there is a salty sea underneath the moon's icy surface. In the 2020s, NASA will send the spacecraft *Europa Clipper* to orbit Europa, one of Jupiter's moons. Like Enceladus, Europa has an icy surface. There might be an ocean of water beneath it. *Europa Clipper* will take pictures and measurements to determine if there could be life on the moon.

Going to Extremes

Even with water, most of Earth's plants and animals could not survive on Mars, Europa, or Enceladus. They are too cold. Temperatures on Mars can reach –195°F (–126°C). Europa and Enceladus are much colder. And these places are filled with other dangers, such as deadly radiation from the sun. How could anything live there?

Extreme temperatures and strong radiation on the surface of Mars mean that most life as we know it would not be able to survive there.

Actually, some creatures might survive in such harsh surroundings. Extremophiles are living things that flourish in places that would kill most other plants and animals. Most extremophiles are single-celled creatures such as bacteria. Some live beneath the bitterly cold ice of Antarctica. Others live near vents in the ocean floor. There, heat from deep inside Earth makes the water boiling hot. If extremophiles can survive such harsh conditions on Earth, they might be able to survive in space.

Scientists study extremophiles to determine if life can exist beyond Earth.

STEM Spotlight

Titan is Saturn's largest moon. It has clouds and rain. It has lakes and seas. But they aren't made of water. They are made of methane. Scientists think that liquid methane, not liquid water, might be the key to life on Titan.

In 2026, NASA will launch a spacecraft named *Dragonfly* (*below*) to explore Titan. The craft will reach Titan in 2034. It will test Titan's air, clouds, ice, land, and oceans to look for signs of life.

Chapter 3

BEYOND THE SOLAR SYSTEM

The universe has billions of stars and planets. Planets in other solar systems are called exoplanets. Since the 1990s, astronomers have identified thousands of exoplanets. Could any of them hold life? Scientists look at an exoplanet's place in space and its features to decide if it's possible.

There are billions of galaxies beyond our own.

The Goldilocks Zone

Earth's place in the solar system makes it ideal for life.
If Earth were closer to the sun, the planet's liquid water
would heat up, boil, and turn into vapor. If Earth were
farther from the sun, all the water would freeze solid.

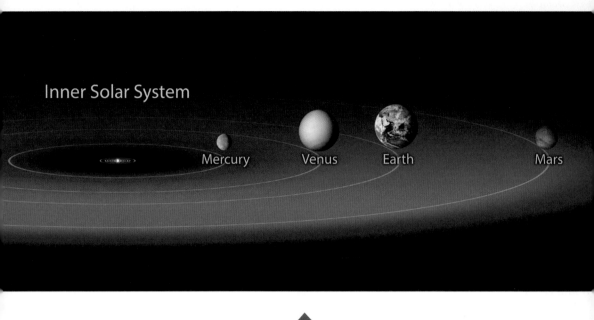

Inner Solar System

Mercury   Venus   Earth   Mars

PLANETS IN THE GOLDILOCKS ZONE (GREEN) ARE THE RIGHT DISTANCE AWAY FROM THEIR STARS TO HAVE LIQUID WATER.

Astronomers say that Earth is in the Goldilocks Zone. The name comes from the fairy tale "Goldilocks and the Three Bears." In the story, Goldilocks tastes three bowls of porridge. One is too hot, one is too cold, and one is "just right." Like the last bowl of porridge, Earth is not too hot or too cold. It is just the right temperature for liquid water.

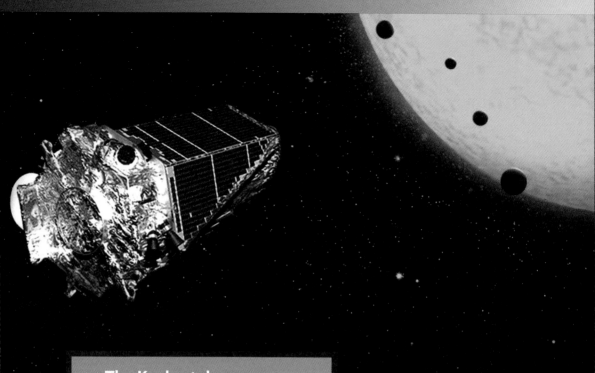

The Kepler telescope was designed to look for planets in or near the Goldilocks Zones of other stars in our galaxy.

Exoplanets are too far away to study with spacecraft. Astronomers study them with telescopes that detect light and other kinds of energy. To find exoplanets that might hold life, astronomers look for ones in the Goldilocks Zones of other stars. These planets are the right distance from their stars to have liquid water.

Planet Protection

Astronomers also look for planets with atmospheres. On Earth, the atmosphere protects living things from dangerous radiation. It also holds the sun's heat, keeping plants and animals warm. The atmosphere also contains oxygen, carbon dioxide, and other gases

Astronomers believe planets with atmospheres are more likely to have life than planets that do not have atmospheres.

K2-18b is currently the only exoplanet known to have water, an atmosphere, and temperatures that could support life.

that living things need to survive. An atmosphere on an exoplanet might be able to protect and support living things in the same way.

A planet called K2-18b travels in the Goldilocks Zone around its star. It is eight times larger than Earth and orbits its star every thirty-three days. Scientists think it has an atmosphere and water. Maybe it holds life.

Fact or fiction?

Tardigrades (*below*) are living on the moon.

This might be true. Tardigrades are extremophiles. In 2007, European researchers sent about three thousand tardigrades into space on the outside of a rocket. The creatures faced extreme cold, powerful radiation, and a lack of water and oxygen. But most of them survived. In April 2019, Israeli scientists sent thousands of tardigrades on a spacecraft to the moon. The craft crash-landed on the moon and couldn't carry out its mission. No one knows whether the tardigrades survived the crash. They might still be alive on the moon.

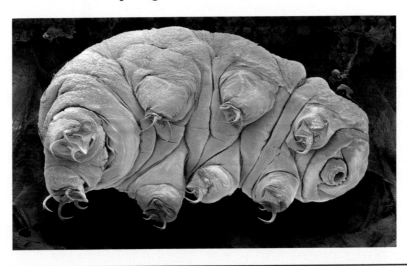

Chapter 4

IS ANYBODY OUT THERE?

The universe has been around for nearly 14 billion years. It has billions of galaxies, and each galaxy has billions of stars and planets. In all that time and space, it seems likely that life has formed someplace other than Earth. Maybe an exoplanet billions of miles from Earth is home to intelligent beings that can communicate, build things, and study the world around them just like humans can.

Life could exist within our own galaxy or within a galaxy far away.

Searching for Extraterrestrials

If the universe is home to other intelligent beings, they could be trying to talk to us. They might be sending radio waves or powerful flashes of light into space, hoping that other intelligent beings will detect them.

THE GREEN BANK TELESCOPE IN WEST VIRGINIA SCANS THE SKIES FOR ALIEN MESSAGES FROM OUTER SPACE.

Most astronomers believe a signal picked up in Ohio in 1977 was caused by a space object, not aliens.

In 1977, a radio telescope called Big Ear in Ohio picked up some superstrong radio waves. They were thirty times more powerful than most radio signals from space. Some people wondered if the signals were a message from aliens. But most scientists think they came from a space object such as a comet.

SETI USES TELESCOPES IN NEW MEXICO AND AROUND THE WORLD.

In 1984, astronomers founded the SETI Institute. SETI stands for the search for extraterrestrial intelligence. The institute runs telescopes around the world. These telescopes scan the skies for signals from extraterrestrial beings.

Hello from Earth

If aliens are out there, they could receive messages from Earth. In 1974, the Arecibo Observatory in Puerto Rico sent a radio message to a group of stars in our galaxy. The message is in binary code, the same system used to program computers. The message shows diagrams of our solar system, a human body, the numbers 1 to 10, and other information about Earth. It will take nearly twenty-five thousand years for the message to reach its destination. If aliens do get our message and reply, it will take another twenty-five thousand years for their signal to reach Earth.

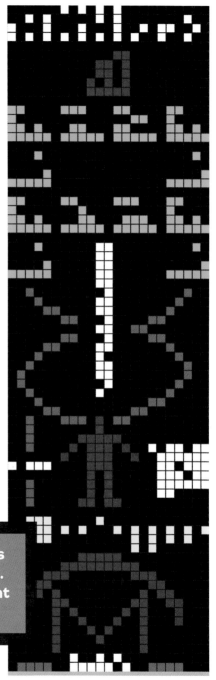

The 1974 Arecibo message is represented here in graphics. Different colors show different pieces of information.

STEM Highlight

In 2019, the Arecibo Observatory (*below*) held a contest asking students to create a message to send to aliens. Teams had to first solve puzzles and unlock coded instructions. Then they had to write a message to aliens about the peaceful uses of space. The teams had to plan how the message would be coded, where in space it would be sent, and what kind of radio signals to use. Dozens of teams have entered the contest. The winning message will be announced in 2020.

The two *Voyager* spacecraft also carry messages from Earth. Launched in 1977, *Voyager 1* and *Voyager 2* studied the outer planets in our solar system. They left the solar system in 2012 and 2018. Each craft carries a golden record containing pictures of Earth and its life-forms, greetings in different languages, music from different cultures, and sounds of nature. An extraterrestrial who played one of the golden records would learn a lot about Earth and humans.

The cover of each golden record gives instructions on how to access the sounds and pictures.

Scientists don't know if there is life somewhere else in the universe, but many of them believe it is unlikely that we are alone. With the help of spacecraft and telescopes, they hope to solve that mystery.

3D Printer Activity

The James Webb Space Telescope will launch in 2021. The telescope will monitor energy from distant galaxies to look for exoplanets. You can download instructions below to make a 3D-printed model of the telescope.

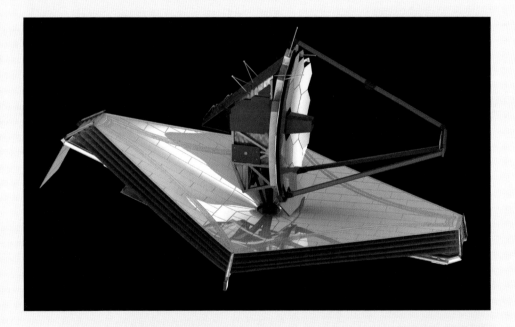

PAGE PLUS

http://qrs.lernerbooks.com/James-Webb

Glossary

atmosphere: a layer of gases surrounding a planet or another body in space

bacteria: tiny one-celled organisms found almost everywhere on Earth

cell: a tiny living thing that can carry on the basic functions of life. All living things are made of at least one cell.

exoplanet: a planet outside our solar system

extraterrestrial: existing outside Earth and its atmosphere. Extraterrestrial is also a term for an alien life-form.

extremophile: a plant, animal, or other living thing that can survive in an extremely cold, extremely hot, or other harsh environment on Earth

galaxy: a system of stars, planets, and other objects in space held together by gravity

radiation: energy that takes the form of waves or tiny particles

radio wave: a type of energy used in many communication devices

solar system: a star, or pair of stars, and the planets and other objects circling around it or them

Learn More about Alien Life

Books

Hamilton, John. Curiosity *Rover: Searching for Life on Mars*. Minneapolis: Abdo, 2018.
Since 2012, the *Curiosity* rover has been looking for signs of life on Mars. Find out what the rover has discovered.

Kenney, Karen Latchana. *Breakthroughs in the Search for Extraterrestrial Life*. Minneapolis: Lerner Publications, 2019.
Learn how scientists are using spacecraft and powerful telescopes to look for life beyond Earth.

Simon, Seymour. *Exoplanets*. New York: HarperCollins, 2018.
This book describes the hunt for exoplanets, especially those that might hold life.

Websites

Extremophile Facts for Kids
https://kids.kiddle.co/Extremophile
Learn more about extremophiles and the strange places they live on Earth.

The New Arecibo Message
http://www.naic.edu/pkg/webutils/challenge/about-challenge.html
Kids from all over the world are competing to create a message to send to extraterrestrial life. Find out more about the contest here.

What Is an Exoplanet?
https://spaceplace.nasa.gov/all-about-exoplanets/en/
This website from NASA describes exoplanets and how scientists look for them.

Index

Photo Acknowledgments

Image credits: Paramount Pictures/Getty Images, p. 4; Ondrej Prosicky/Shutterstock.com, p. 5; STEVE GSCHMEISSNER/SCIENCE PHOTO LIBRARY/Getty Images, p. 6; Kees Smans/ Moment/Getty Images, p. 7; NASA/Ames/JPL-Caltech, p. 8; NASA/JPL-Caltech/MSSS, p. 9; NASA/JPL-Caltech/Space Science Institute, p. 10; NASA/JPL-Caltech/University of Arizona, p. 11; Markus Matzel/ullstein bild/Getty Images, p. 13; NASA, p. 13; NASA/Goddard, p. 14; NASA, p. 15; NASA/Getty Images, p. 16; NASA/Ames/JPL-Caltech/T Pyle, p. 17; ESA and A.Vidal-Madjar, p. 18; ESA/Hubble, p. 19; STEVE GSCHMEISSNER/SCIENCE PHOTO LIBRARY/ Getty Images, p. 20; NASA/ESA Hubble Space Telescope, p. 21; ANDREW CABALLERO-REYNOLDS/AFP/Getty Images, p. 22; Harpazo Hope/Moment/Getty Images, p. 23; Zack Frank/Shutterstock.com, p. 24; Arne Nordmann/Wikimedia Commons (CC BY-SA 3.0), p. 25; Bettmann/Getty Images, p. 26; Great Images in NASA/Wikimedia Commons (Public Domain), p. 27 (right); Nasa/Wikimedia Commons (Public Domain), p. 27 (left); M2 Photography/Alamy Stock Photo, p. 28; alex-mit/iStock/Getty Images, p. 29.

Cover: Yuga Kurita/Moment/Getty Images.